Feltlicious

needle-felted treats to make & give

Text by Kari Chapin
Projects Designed and Created by Kerri \

sixth&springbooks
New York

D1441592

sixth&springbooks

161 Avenue of the Americas, New York, NY 10013
sixthandspringbooks.com

Editorial Director
JOY AQUILINO

Vice President
TRISHA MALCOLM

Developmental Editor
LISA SILVERMAN

Publisher
CARRIE KILMER

Art Director
DIANE LAMPHRON

Production Manager
DAVID JOINNIDES

Page Designer
ARETA BUK

President
ART JOINNIDES

Editorial Assistant
JOHANNA LEVY

Chairman
JAY STEIN

Copyeditor
ALISON HAGGE

Proofreader
KRISTIN M. JONES

Project Photography
JACK DEUTSCH

Stylists
KRISTINE TREVINO
DIANE LAMPHRON

Step Photography
KERRI WESSEL

DEDICATIONS

We would like to dedicate
this book to our family and friends.
Thank you for your support and
encouragement while we worked
on this incredible project.
—Kari & Kerri

I'd like to dedicate
my part of this book to my
wonderful co-author, Kerri.
Here's to the start of something
sweet, my friend.
—Kari

Text copyright © 2013 by Kari Chapin and Kerri Wessel

Felted food, project designs, and step-by-step
photography copyright © 2013 by Kerri Wessel

Photography of completed foods and projects
copyright © 2013 by Soho Publishing, LLC

Coke™ and the Coke™ glass are trademarks of the
Coca-Cola Company.

Cataloging-in-Publication Data is available from
the Library of Congress.

ISBN: 978-1-936096-64-0

Manufactured in China

1 3 5 7 9 10 8 6 4 2

First Edition

Contents

Pancakes with Syrup
page 25

Fried Egg, Bacon & Toast
page 28

Toaster Pastry
page 35

Baguette
page 38

Croissant
page 41

Grilled Cheese Sandwich
page 45

Hot Dog
page 48

Cheeseburger & Root Beer Float
page 52

Cup o' Joe
page 59

Strawberry
page 63

Peach Half
page 67

Avocado Half
page 70

Watermelon Wedge
page 74

Carrot
page 78

Cut Lime
page 82

Apple Half
page 85

Vanilla Ice
Cream Cone
page 89

Chocolate Chip
Cookie
page 92

Frosted Cake Slice
page 96

Frosted Cupcake
page 99

Chocolate-Covered
Doughnut
page 102

Macaron
page 105

Cherry Pie Slice
page 107

Valentine's
Lollipop
page 111

Dark Chocolate
Bunny
page 114

Rocket Pop
page 117

Candy Corn
page 120

Pumpkin Pie Slice
page 123

Iced Gingerbread
Man
page 126

Apple Pendant
page 130

Rocket Pop Key Chain
page 131

Watermelon Pin
page 132

Heart Lollipop
Headband
page 133

Bacon Strip Magnet
page 134

Cup o' Joe
Paperweight
page 135

Peach Wall Hanging
page 136

Root Beer Float
Pincushion
page 137

Easter Bunny
Centerpiece
page 138

Frosted Cake Slice
Place Card Holder
page 139

Gingerbread Man
Ornament
page 140

Preface

Hello, friend! We're Kerri Wessel and Kari Chapin, and we're happy to have the opportunity to share our love of both needle felting and food with you.

Why felted food? The answer is easy! Everyone can relate to it on any number of levels, from nostalgia to everyday cravings. Crafting provides at least two things for many people—comfort and a creative outlet—so it just made sense to us to combine the two. The wonderful thing about using food as a model is it's so easy to make it your own. Here's what you can look forward to on your needle-felting adventures:

You'll enjoy total crafting freedom. Even if you're following one of our recipes, there's no way you can go wrong. Even if you're nearly done you can still make big changes. Want to change the color of something? Simply lay the new color over the old and felt it down. It's almost as if you can erase your mistakes, simply by adding more wool.

It's cost effective. No expensive supplies are necessary. Even the start-up costs are low. A general needle-felting kit, with enough wool to make several projects in this book, will cost less than thirty-five dollars. Needle-felting supplies can be found in craft stores and online. See Resources (page 141) for ideas on where to begin.

There are no creative limits. You can make jewelry, fashion embellishments, gifts, and useful items for your home. We've provided lots of ideas for turning any of your felted foods into any of the projects.

It's easy. You can take your needle felting with you anywhere you would take a book or your knitting. It's easy to teach older children to needle felt too. Just make sure they understand how to use the needles safely and keep an eye on them while they work.

We both hope that you come to enjoy this medium as much as we do. The sky's the limit, and we'd love to see what you make. Share your images with us at pinterest.com/kerriwessel/feltlicious/.

Thanks so much, and happy felting!

Kerri & Kari

Tools & Techniques

Basic Supplies

If you're new to needle felting you don't need much to get started. With just a few very affordable tools, you'll soon be on your way. You may even have some things lying around your home, and some tools you can make yourself if you'd like. Let's get started! Here's what you'll need.

WOOL

Wool is a wonderful medium. Any type of loose wool will work for our projects. As you investigate sources, you'll find that wool is very affordable. We think it's a worthwhile investment for you to try various types of fibers, then decide what you like best. In most cases you can buy wool by the ounce.

Wool is sold in several different forms. For the projects in this book, we used either batting or roving. **Batting** is wool that's been carded (cleaned and combed), but the direction of its fibers is all mixed up, and the natural crimp of the wool is still visible. **Roving,** which is usually sold in long strips, is more thoroughly carded than batting, so its fibers are smoother, flatter, and generally aligned in the same direction. Roving can need some finessing when using it to felt a three-dimensional project, so it's best to begin by fluffing it up to give it more body. You can easily do this by gently pulling the fibers apart and teasing the wool a bit with your fingers.

Raw wool is wool that has been shorn from the sheep but hasn't been cleaned or carded. If you choose to use raw wool, you'll need to clean it by first removing any debris, then washing it. You can also dye raw wool.

For all the projects in this book a slightly coarse wool was used, either C1 or Corriedale. **C1** is a specialty wool blend consisting of shorter fibers, which some

Batting (top) is wool that's been carded, but its fibers aren't as smooth as they are in roving (bottom), which is wool that's even more thoroughly carded.

felters believe make it easier to felt. **Corriedale** fibers (from the Corriedale sheep) are a bit longer than the ones in C1 wool, which can give you a smoother finish, but Corriedale can take longer to felt.

Sometimes you'll hear people talk about **core wool.** This is simply a less expensive wool, usually one that's undyed and sometimes contains bits of natural matter (like bits of sticks) that needle felters use for the insides of larger projects. Our projects are small, so we don't use core wool, but as you experiment more with needle felting you may find that you want to use core wool to explore creating projects of different shapes and sizes.

Store your wool in an airtight container or bag. Moths love wool, and you'll want to keep them away from yours.

FELTING NEEDLES

Needles for felting come in a few different sizes and shapes. The important thing to remember is that needles made for felting have barbs at the pointy ends. These are what actually felt the wool. The barbs catch the fibers in the wool and tangle them together, which is what eventually causes shapes and other details to form.

There are two basic needle shapes: **Triangle-shaped needles** have barbs on all three sides, while **star-shaped needles** have more sides and, therefore, more barbs.

The number on the needle is a gauge. The lower the number, the thicker the needle. You'll need a range of sizes, because a larger (or thicker) needle will be harder to get through your wool once it's been compacted, but it can be useful in the beginning to get things into shape fast. To get started, we recommend the following four needles:

38 Star. The shaft of this needle is on the thin side, which means it creates a smooth felted surface. Its star shapes gives it extra barbs, which makes it a fast felter too.

36 Triangle. The thickest needle in our toolbox, this is a great choice for starting a project because it grabs a lot of fiber with each poke.

38 Triangle. This needle is good for finishing your projects. It doesn't grab a lot of wool, just tiny tufts. It's not the best for shaping, but it's great for getting a smooth surface.

40 Triangle. This needle is good for your finest detail work and for smoothing down any stray fibers.

All four of these general-purpose felting needles are easy to find and affordable. The different types and sizes of needles are color coded, but you should keep in mind that the colors aren't standardized. The colors used to identify type and size will vary depending on where and from whom you buy your needles.

Needles can break easily if you're too hard on them, so stock up. It's also possible for the needles to get a bit dull. You'll know when it's happening because they'll become less effective. You'll be able to feel the difference—it's harder to push a dull needle through the wool. Simply replace them when you need to.

MULTI-NEEDLE TOOLS

Multiple-needle tools are very helpful, as they can save you a lot of time. Kerri uses them as often as she can. She loads 38 Stars into her multi-needle tools. At the beginning of your project, when you're working on your general shape and getting the middle done, this tool will help your work go a lot faster. Not all needles fit in all multi-needle tools, so make sure the tool you buy is a match for the needles you have.

Our favorite multi-needle tool is made by Clover and it holds three needles. Kerri made her own five-needle tool, and you can too!

Four types of felting needles—from top, a 38 Star, a 36 Triangle, a 38 Triangle, and a 40 Triangle—a Clover multi-needle tool (right), and one of Kerri's homemade multi-needle tools (below).

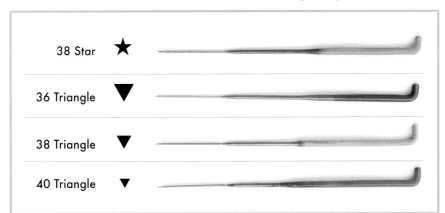

38 Star	★	
36 Triangle	▼	
38 Triangle	▼	
40 Triangle	▼	

MAKING YOUR OWN MULTI-NEEDLE TOOL

At your local craft supply retailer, look for a wooden candleholder, one with a small, hollow wooden shape and a rounded top. You can also buy (or reuse) a cork that will fit snugly into the opening of the candleholder. Once you're home, use a drill with a bit just slightly larger than your needles (you need a tight fit) and drill at least five holes into the cork, spaced evenly apart. Imagine a square in the middle of your cork, drill a hole on each corner, then drill in the center of the square. Then simply put the needles of your choice into the drilled holes and secure the cork into the candleholder. Voilà! You now have a custom multi-needle tool. Kerri uses her homemade tool for 38 Stars.

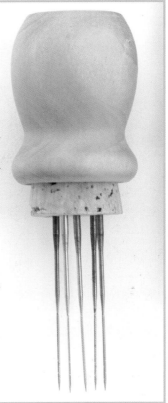

A few basic but essential needle felting tools: a work surface (a flannel-covered foam mat is shown here), two pet brushes that are used as carders, and a small pair of sharp scissors.

WORK SURFACE

When you're needle felting, you need a work surface. That way, you can lay your piece on your mat, hold it in place with your hand, and poke down toward your work surface with your felting needle, rather than poking your piece while it's in your hand. We don't recommend that you felt your piece away from your work surface unless it's absolutely necessary. Two choices of work surfaces are available.

Brush mat. These are usually small mats with a sort of bristle top—not unlike a scrub brush, but softer.

High-density foam mat. You can buy thick, high-density foam at many craft or fabric supply stores. If the piece of foam you buy is too large, you can cut it to the size you'd like with an electric knife. We like mats that are 9 x 12"/23 x 30.5cm the best. We recommend that you cover the foam with a piece of flannel. This will prevent your project from felting into the foam and will also keep any bits of foam out of your project. Also, the flannel will allow your foam to last longer and will be easier to clean.

CARDERS

When mixing colors of wool, which we highly recommend you do, you'll need to card it. The least expensive tool to use for doing this is a pet brush. Yes, that's right—a simple pet brush. Look for one that has hard, well-spaced bristles. We talk more about using these to blend colors on page 20.

Professional hand carders are also available, as well as big drum carders, but unless you get very, very serious about blending larger batches of wool, you'll be fine sticking with the inexpensive pet brush variety.

OTHER SUPPLIES

These are a few other items you'll need to make the needle-felting process easier.

Scale. Wool doesn't weigh very much, so you'll need a scale that can measure in grams to get the most accurate measurement. In our instructions we use grams to give you an idea of how much of each color we use to create each food. You can buy a basic kitchen scale at most home goods stores. For more information on measuring wool, see page 12.

Bristled hairbrush. This is used for cleaning the flannel on a foam work surface when you change colors of the wool. Any inexpensive nylon bristle brush will do.

Thimbles. These are optional. No matter how careful you are when you're working, you'll poke yourself. It's unavoidable. A thimble might help protect your fingers. Having a few Band-Aids on hand isn't a bad idea, either. But nothing will help you as much as keeping your eyes on your work.

Scissors. It's handy to have a pair of embroidery scissors to snip errant fibers from your finished products. You may also find yourself needing to cut into wool for some of the projects, and so it'll be important to have a pair of scissors that you can wield comfortably. Make sure your scissors are sharp!

Desk lamp. A bright desk lamp is a must for the technique we use to create highlights on projects (see page 22).

General Techniques

As we've said before, there is no wrong way to create a needle-felted project. As you become more comfortable with the general process of working in this medium, you'll begin to find the methods that work best for you. We've included our tips and tricks here, but remember to do what feels and looks best to you.

MEASURING WOOL

To create the projects in this book, we weighed our wool using a scale that measures in grams and provided those amounts in the recipes to help you get an idea of where to begin. But there are other ways to judge how much wool you'll need to use for any project you want to make.

If you gather up the wool you think you'll need for a project and squeeze it tightly in your hands, you'll wind up with a good approximation of what size your finished project will be. If you want the project to be larger, add more wool. If you want a smaller project, just take some wool away.

We also use the terms **tuft** (about the size of your palm) and **pinch** (about what you can hold between your thumb and two forefingers) in the ingredients lists. (For visual reference, see the photo below.) Use your best judgment for these amounts, and keep in mind that all weights and measurements are suggestions because everyone felts their projects a bit differently.

A pinch (left) and a tuft (right) of wool shown at actual size.

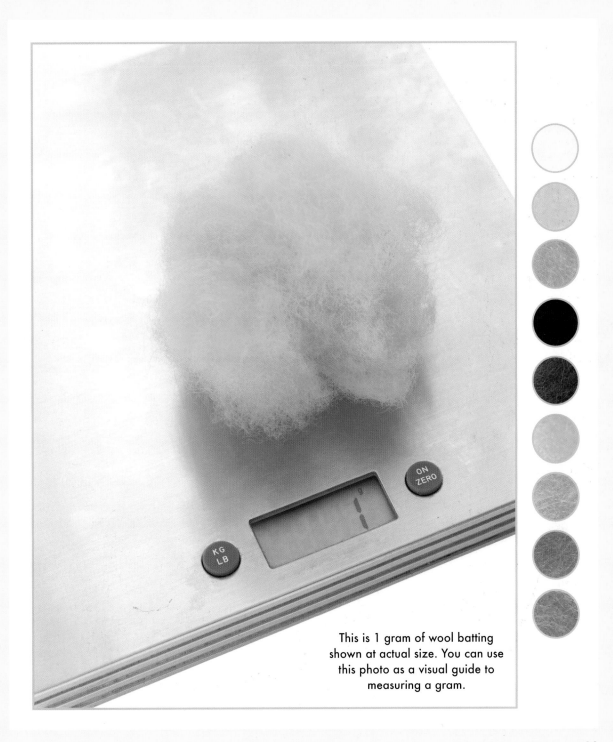

This is 1 gram of wool batting shown at actual size. You can use this photo as a visual guide to measuring a gram.

NEEDLE-FELTING BASICS

Needle felting is wonderful and very satisfying. It's easy enough to just jump in and begin. It's important to know that there's no "right" or "wrong" when needle felting. You simply decide what you'd like to create and then you begin sculpting. The loose wool is easy to manipulate and the needles are easy to handle.

The main thing to remember when poking or jabbing your wool is that you need to go straight in and straight out. You can enter the wool from any direction, but just be sure that you go in and pull out straight. If you twist the needle while you're working, chances are the needle will break off inside your project. That's not the end of the world, but it'll make finishing your project a bit harder.

How can you tell when you're done? The answer is simple: whenever you're pleased with your project. It's all a matter of personal taste. We like our projects to be hard and tight, which we feel is better for holding their shape and working with a lot of detail. Your work will get harder and tighter the longer you felt it. Also, the more you felt something the smaller it gets, so keep that in mind while you work as well.

When we're finished with a project, we like to go over it with very thin tufts of wool and a smaller needle, like a 40 Triangle. This process helps to smooth out the surface and cover any deep needle holes.

To "erase" a mistake (such as when you've felted a groove too deeply), simply take a tuft of wool and carefully felt it into the groove until you're satisfied.

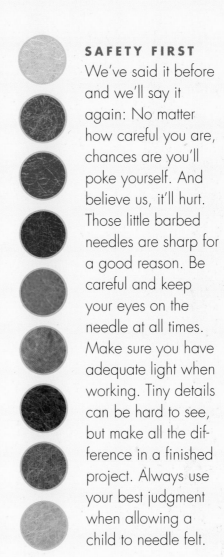

SAFETY FIRST

We've said it before and we'll say it again: No matter how careful you are, chances are you'll poke yourself. And believe us, it'll hurt. Those little barbed needles are sharp for a good reason. Be careful and keep your eyes on the needle at all times. Make sure you have adequate light when working. Tiny details can be hard to see, but make all the difference in a finished project. Always use your best judgment when allowing a child to needle felt.

MAKING BASIC SHAPES

Before we move on to the projects, we want to talk a bit about basic shapes. Most of our projects use these shapes, so they're a good place to begin practicing. You can always refer to this section if questions pop up when you're working on a project.

Cylinders: Rocket Pop and Baguette

Rectangles: Toaster Pastry and Toast

Wedges: Grilled Cheese and Candy Corn

CYLINDER

Lay out the wool in a long strip.

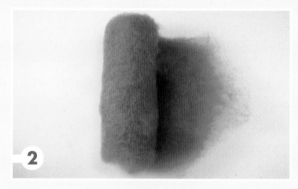

Beginning at one end, tightly roll up the strip and felt down the end of the strip to secure it.

Felt the ends of the cylinder until they're flat, then felt the entire surface, turning the piece often to make sure you work it evenly.

RECTANGLE

Lay out the wool in a long strip and felt over the entire surface to flatten and compact it.

Beginning at one end, fold the strip over on itself from one end to the other, working from left to right.

Felt the ends and sides of the rectangle until they're flat, then felt the entire surface. Continue to re-flatten the sides as you work to keep the corners sharp.

WEDGE OR TRIANGLE FOLD

Lay out the wool in a long strip.

Fold the corner of one end to the opposite edge to create a triangle. Repeat until you reach the end of your strip. Lightly felt the edge to secure.

Refine the triangle into a wedge by flattening the sides and rounding the bottom of the wedge as you felt it, then felt the entire surface.

SPHERE

1

Begin by gathering the wool into a loose ball and felting it into place.

2

Continue to felt and refine the sphere, turning constantly as you work.

Spheres: Apple and Macaron

SELECTING COLORS

In our recipes we use color names to describe the colors we've chosen. We've provided a color chart opposite to give you an idea of what those colors look like. The wool you buy may not exactly match what we've used, and that's fine. You'll have a very clear idea of what we consider "Rose" or "Kiwi," and as long as the wool you choose is a close enough match, your projects will resemble ours. But don't limit yourself to our choices, and don't hesitate to make these projects your own—there are so many wonderful colors of wool in the world, and it's fun to see and choose what you like best. Personalizing these projects will ensure that you really enjoy a sense of freedom when you're felting. To inspire you, we included wonderful artists in the Resources listing (see page 141) so you can see some of the many ways that color can be used in needle-felted projects.

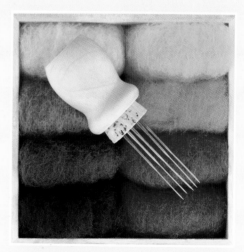

PALE PINK

TANGERINE

LEMON LIME

TAUPE

ROSE

OCHER

KIWI

LIGHT BROWN

RED

MARIGOLD

MOSS GREEN

PELSULL OCHER

BRICK RED

LEMON

CARIBBEAN SEA

CHOCOLATE

SCARLET

PALE YELLOW

DUSTY ROSE

ESPRESSO

BUFF

NATURAL WHITE

BRIGHT WHITE

BLENDING COLORS

Blending colors is easy, but it's not an exact science. Kerri blended wool for almost every single one of our projects, and she likes to get as close to the natural color of the food as possible, but you don't have to approach projects this way if you don't want to. If you want a bright red slice of watermelon, go for it! There is no wrong way to do any of these projects.

If your project calls for 8 grams of a color mixture, start with smaller amounts of each color and add as you blend. Start by blending a little bit of each color, and keep adding and blending until you have the amount you need and a color combination you like. The colors listed for each project are the combinations of colors that Kerri uses, and while we supply total weights of a mixed color to use for scale, it's all approximate and open to your own interpretation.

It's easiest to begin blending your colors by hand. Take tufts of each color and hold them together with the ends in each hand. Gently pull the fibers apart and into two pieces by moving your hands away from each other. Lay your pieces back on top of each other and repeat this process until your colors begin to mix.

To further blend your wool, you'll need those two pet brushes we mentioned earlier (see page 11).

The brushes can only handle a small amount of wool at a time, so you'll have to mix your color in batches.

Lay a small amount of your partially mixed wool on the bristles of one of your brushes with the fibers lined up parallel to the brush handle. Hold this brush in your left hand face up. Holding your other brush in your right hand, brush your fiber brush from the handle end of the bristles to the front edge of the brush (see photo 1). Continue to do this until all of the fibers are transferred from one brush to the other and then switch hands and repeat until your colors are fully blended.

The most basic use for blending colors is to use two or more colors to make a third color, as seen in photo 2, where we've used red and yellow wool to make an orange.

By varying the proportions of the colors you begin with, you can mix up nearly any color in the rainbow. As shown in photo 3, try adding more of one wool or the other to see how many varieties you can make from just two basic colors.

3

Another great use for blending your colors is to create a smooth transition from one color to the next as shown in photo 4, which can come in handy for illuminating your projects (see page 22) or creating the subtle shifts in color you might find in the blush of an apple or the skin of a peach.

4

ILLUMINATING YOUR PROJECTS

You'll notice as you look at our projects that Kerri uses a lot of color gradations and highlights. These details really make her work shine. Illuminating your projects is optional, but it will really help put your projects over the top.

To create highlights, place your project in bright light from a lamp. The light that hits your project needs to come from one direction, so place your project in the pool of light, not directly underneath the lamp. Try placing your project in different spots—to the right or to the left of the light source—to see what kind of results you get.

When placing the wool on the spots you want to illuminate, work lightly. It's easier to add more wool if you need to, but very hard to take it away. Pull the fibers apart with your fingers to create a fine web of fibers. Needle these carefully to the spot you want to illuminate, and slowly add more fiber if you want to emphasize them. Remember, it's easy to add fiber, but harder to take it away, so go slowly and keep checking your work under your lamp.

CREATING HIGHLIGHTS

This illustration shows how highlights work. Each area of the highlight gradually gets smaller while also becoming lighter. The lightest area is the smallest.

Light Source

White (only add white to your highlight if the surface is meant to look shiny)

Second Value

First Value

Base Color

To keep the highlights looking natural, layer different values of similar hues, one on top of another. **Hue** is the actual color, such as red or blue, and **value** refers to a color's lightness or darkness.

The detail photos of three projects—a glistening Fried Egg (see page 29), a bumpy Carrot (page 78) and a soft Croissant (page 41)—show how highlights are used on different kinds of surfaces.

Good Morning

BREAKFAST BAR

PANCAKES WITH SYRUP

FRIED EGG, BACON & TOAST

TOASTER PASTRY

BAGUETTE

CROISSANT

Pancakes with Syrup

If you're uncomfortable with your ability to make a circle, try using a biscuit cutter instead of making this freestyle. Simply pick a cutter in your desired size, layer the wool in the cutter, and felt it into a compact shape. But remember—homemade pancakes are never perfect circles either!

SUPPLIES

Basic tools (see pages 8–11)

Optional: Biscuit or circle cookie cutter, if desired

INGREDIENTS

To make a stack of pancakes with syrup and a pat of butter

7 grams of an Ocher and Pale Yellow blend (for the pancakes)

1 gram of a Pale Yellow and Buff blend (for the pancake edges)

1 tuft of a Chocolate and Ocher blend (for the syrup)

1 pinch each of Ocher and Pale Yellow (for the syrup highlights)

1 tuft of a Marigold and Lemon blend (for the pat of butter)

1 pinch each of Pale Yellow and Bright White (for the butter highlights)

PANCAKE STACK

1. Thoroughly blend the Ocher and Pale Yellow. Lay out the blended wool in a 4 x 12"/10.2 x 30.5cm strip.

2. Fold the strip over to form a 4"/10.2cm square. Continue to fold the strip over onto itself until you reach the end, then lightly felt the whole square.

3. Round the corners of the square by felting each in toward the center.

4. Work all four corners until you're left with a squat cylinder. These are your pancakes.

5. Felt a deep groove in the center of the side of the cylinder, working all the way around the pancake stack.

PANCAKE EDGES

6. Thoroughly blend the Pale Yellow and Buff. Roll two long strips of the blended wool between your palms and felt each around the edge of your pancake stack— one above and one below the groove.

SYRUP

7. Thoroughly blend the Chocolate and Ocher. Take a tuft of the blended wool and felt it to the top of your pancakes. Use the tip of your needle to "draw"

interesting shapes around the edge of your syrup as you felt it into place.

ILLUMINATE YOUR SYRUP

8. Following the guidelines on page 22, use Ocher and Pale Yellow to add highlights to your syrup.

PAT OF BUTTER; ILLUMINATE YOUR BUTTER

9. Thoroughly blend the Marigold and Lemon. Roll a small ball of the blended wool and felt it into place on top of your syrup. Flatten the edges into a square as you felt the pat of butter into place. Following the guidelines on page 22, use Pale Yellow and Bright White to add highlights to the pat of butter. ∎

Fried Egg, Bacon & Toast

The fried egg is made in two separate pieces that you'll felt together. Felt the yolk onto the egg white from underneath, because the white piece is thin. By doing it this way, the colors will be less likely to poke through. Getting your bacon crispy (or wavy) is easily done. However, getting the bacon strip to hold its shape will take some extra felting. Just keep flipping your bacon strip and working both sides evenly.

SUPPLIES

Basic tools (see pages 8–11)

Fried Egg

INGREDIENTS

To make one fried egg

5 grams of Natural White (for the egg white)

1 gram of a Lemon and Marigold blend (for the yolk)

1 pinch each of Pale Yellow and Bright White (for the yolk highlights)

EGG WHITE

1. Lay out your natural white wool in a 3 x 9"/7.6 x 22.9cm strip and felt over the entire surface lightly.

2. Fold the strip over upon itself, working from one end to the other, until you're left with a square that's approximately 3 x 3"/7.6 x 7.6cm. Felt the entire surface of the square lightly.

3. Round the corners of your square by felting each corner in toward the center.

YOLK

4. Thoroughly blend the Lemon and Marigold. Felt this blended wool to create a sphere, then flatten one side to form the yolk.

5. Attach the flattened side of your yolk to your egg white by felting from the back, being careful not to poke the white wool through the yolk.

ILLUMINATE YOUR YOLK

6. Following the guidelines on page 22, use pinches of Pale Yellow and Bright White to illuminate your yolk. ■

Bacon Strip

INGREDIENTS

To make one strip of bacon

4 grams of a Brick Red, Ocher, and Scarlet blend (for the main body)

1 tuft of a Buff and Ocher blend (for the fat)

1 pinch each of Ocher and Natural White (for the highlights)

MAIN BODY

1. Thoroughly blend the Brick Red, Ocher, and Scarlet. Lay out the blended wool in a 3½ x 9"/8.9 x 22.9cm strip. Lightly felt the entire surface.

2. Fold the strip over about 1"/2.5cm. Continue to fold it over until you have a strip that's about 3½ x 1½"/8.9 x 3.8cm. Felt the strip until it's firm.

3. Felt a deep groove down the middle of the bacon strip. Flip the strip over and felt two additional deep grooves, one between each end of the strip and the center.

4. Now you're going to make the ripples. Working on the side with the two grooves, tip your bacon strip up on its end and press it down lightly on the foam pad. Holding your piece at this angle, felt into the grooves and the ends of the strip to hold the ripples in place.

FAT

5. Thoroughly blend the Buff and Ocher. Roll two strips of the blended wool in your palms to create the fat and position them lengthwise along both sides of the bacon strip. Felt them into place.

ILLUMINATE YOUR BACON

6. Following the guidelines on page 22, use Ocher to add highlights to the meat and Natural White to add highlights to the fat. ■

Buttered Toast

INGREDIENTS

To make one piece of buttered toast

6 grams of a Pale Yellow and Buff blend (for the main body)

1 gram of an Ocher and Chocolate blend (for the crust and burn lines)

1 small tuft of a Pale Yellow, Marigold, and Lemon blend (for the melted butter)

1 tuft of a Marigold and Lemon blend (for the pat of butter)

1 pinch each of Pale Yellow and Bright White (for the butter highlights)

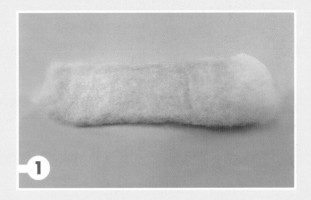

MAIN BODY

1. Thoroughly blend the Pale Yellow and Buff. Lay out the blended wool in a 3 x 12"/7.6 x 30.5cm strip and felt the whole strip lightly.

2. Fold the strip over itself from one end to the other until you're left with a 3 x 3"/7.6 x 7.6cm square. Felt the piece of bread until it's firm.

CRUST

3. Thoroughly blend the Ocher and Chocolate; set aside a tuft for your burn lines. Roll a strip between your palms, wrap it all the way around the edge of your bread, and felt it into place.

4. Felt two deep grooves into the sides of your bread about one-third of the way down from the top, then round the top corners.

BURN LINES

5. Roll three thin strips of the reserved blend you created in Step 3, lay them lengthwise down the back of your toast, and felt into place.

BUTTER; ILLUMINATE YOUR BUTTER

6. For the melted butter, thoroughly blend the Pale Yellow, Marigold, and Lemon. Take a thin tuft of the blended wool, gently pull it apart with your fingers like a spiderweb, spread it on the surface of your bread, then felt until it's flat. Make your butter layer thin—you can always add more if you desire. For the pat of butter, thoroughly blend the Marigold and Lemon. Roll the blended wool into a small ball and tack it onto the surface of your toast. Refine the ball into a square pat by flattening the sides as you felt it down. Following the guidelines on page 22, use Pale Yellow and Bright White to add highlights. ■

Toaster Pastry

You can make any flavor of toaster pastry you'd like. Instead of using white frosting, try pink wool for strawberry. Or switch up the filling and use blue wool to make blueberry.

SUPPLIES
Basic tools (see pages 8–11)

INGREDIENTS
To make one toaster pastry

8 grams of a Pale Yellow and Ocher blend (for the main body)

1 tuft of Ocher (for the holes on back)

1 gram of Natural White (for the icing)

1 tuft of Scarlet (for the filling)

1 pinch each of Tangerine, Marigold, and Pale Yellow (for the filling highlights)

Pinches of Kiwi, Marigold, Scarlet, Pale Pink, and Tangerine (for the sprinkles)

MAIN BODY

1. Thoroughly blend the Pale Yellow and Ocher. Lay out the blended wool in a 4 x 8"/10.2 x 20.4cm strip and felt over the entire surface.

2. Fold the strip over upon itself, working from one end to the other until you're left with a rectangle that's approximately 4 x 3"/10.2 x 7.6cm.

3. Continue to refine your toaster pastry, flattening each side and trying to keep the corners sharp.

4. Felt a flat, ¼"/6.4mm border around the edge of your toaster pastry. To create the pinched edge of the

pastry, felt deep, evenly spaced grooves all the way around the flattened border.

HOLES ON BACK

5. Flip your toaster pastry over. Roll eight small balls of Ocher between your fingertips, then felt them onto the back of your toaster pastry in straight, evenly spaced lines.

ICING

6. Cover the center of the front of your toaster pastry with Natural White and felt over the whole surface. Use the tip of your needle to "draw" interesting shapes around the edge as you felt it down.

FILLING

7. Cut off one corner of your toaster pastry.

8. Take the tuft of Scarlet and roll a short strip between your palms. Cover the cut corner of your toaster pastry with the strip and felt it into place.

ILLUMINATE YOUR TOASTER PASTRY; ADD SPRINKLES

9. Following the guidelines on page 22, use Tangerine, Marigold, and Pale Yellow to add highlights to the filling. For the sprinkles, roll tiny pinches of Kiwi, Marigold, Scarlet, Pale Pink, and Tangerine into little strips and felt them onto the icing. ■

Baguette

We illuminated the crust on our baguette by placing a lamp to the left of our project. Where the light hit the strongest on the baguette is where we added our highlights. Trying this trick at home will make your creation look as if it's fresh from the oven.

SUPPLIES

Basic tools (see pages 8–11)

INGREDIENTS

To make one baguette

8 grams of a Pale Yellow and Buff blend (for the main body)

1 gram of a Pale Yellow and Ocher blend (for the crust)

1 pinch each of Pale Yellow and Natural White (for the highlights)

MAIN BODY

1. Thoroughly blend the Pale Yellow and Buff. Lay out the blended wool in a 4 x 8"/10.2 x 20.4cm strip. Beginning at one end, roll up the strip as tightly as possible into a thin cylinder and secure the ends. Lightly felt the entire surface.

2. Felt the ends of the cylinder into slightly rounded, tapered points.

3. Continue to refine the shape, making your baguette as symmetrical as you can.

CRUST

4. Thoroughly blend the Pale Yellow and Ocher, reserving a tuft of the mixture for Step 5. Cover the sides and bottom of the baguette with the blended wool, stopping about halfway up the sides and leaving the middle of the top of the baguette exposed. Felt the crust into place.

5. Take the blended wool that you reserved from Step 4 and form two strips, each approximately ½"/1.3cm wide. Lay the strips across the exposed middle section of the baguette and felt them into place. Once the strips are felted into place, accentuate the strips of crust by indenting the lighter exposed areas in between.

ILLUMINATE YOUR BAGUETTE

6. Following the guidelines on page 22, use Pale Yellow and Natural White to add highlights to your crust. ■

Croissant

Giving the wool a push in the right direction can help you form your pieces. In this project, for example, we begin with a basic cylinder, but the magic happens when you modify it with your fingers. To bring the points of the croissant closer, you need to push the wool inward. This is one of the amazing qualities of working with wool—it bends to your will!

SUPPLIES

Basic tools (see pages 8–11)

INGREDIENTS

To make one croissant

5 grams of a Pale Yellow and Ocher blend (for the main body)

1 tuft of an Ocher and Chocolate blend (for the browning)

1 tuft of Pale Yellow (for the edge highlights)

MAIN BODY

1. Thoroughly blend the Pale Yellow and Ocher. Separate out 1 gram and save it for later.

2. Lay out the blended wool in a 4 x 8"/10.2 x 20.4cm strip.

3. Beginning at one end, roll up the wool as tightly as possible into a cylinder and secure the end. Then lightly felt the entire surface.

4. Continue to refine the shape by felting both ends of the cylinder into tapered points.

5. Gently pinch the ends of the cylinder in toward each other as though folding it in half. Holding it

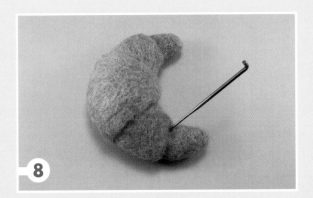

in this position with your thumb and forefinger while you work, felt your piece *carefully* until it holds a crescent shape on its own. Felt out any folds or creases in the crescent shape.

6. Use the gram of blended wool you set aside in Step 1 to form a flat isosceles triangle, leaving the bottom loose along the edge.

7. Place the tip of the triangle in the middle of the inside curve of your croissant and tack it into place. Wrap the loose edge of the triangle around to the back of your croissant and felt it flat.

8. Felt a deep groove halfway between the edge of the triangle and one end of your croissant. Continue to work the end of your croissant from the groove down to the tip until it's slightly smaller in size than the section from the groove to the triangle. Repeat this process on the other side so the croissant is symmetrical.

BROWNING AND HIGHLIGHTS

9. Thoroughly blend the Ocher and Chocolate. Wrap your croissant in thin, wispy pieces of this mixture and felt the entire surface. Using Pale Yellow, add highlights to the edges of the layers of your croissant (see page 22 for guidelines). ∎

Diner Delights

TODAY'S SPECIALS

GRILLED CHEESE SANDWICH

HOT DOG

CHEESEBURGER &
ROOT BEER FLOAT

CUP O' JOE

Grilled Cheese Sandwich

This is a great project to consider adding some extra elements to. How about a bit of bacon peeking out between the slices of bread, or maybe a slice of tomato? Refer to our cheeseburger project (see page 52) for ideas on adding your favorite toppings.

SUPPLIES
Basic tools (see pages 8–11)

INGREDIENTS
To make two halves of a grilled cheese sandwich

12 grams of a Pale Yellow and Buff blend (for the main body)

1 gram of an Ocher and Chocolate blend (for the crust)

1 gram of a Tangerine and Marigold blend (for the cheese)

4 tufts of Ocher (for the toasting)

1 pinch each of Lemon and Pale Yellow (for the cheese highlights)

MAIN BODY

1. Thoroughly blend the Pale Yellow and Buff. Lay out half of the blended wool in a 3 x 8"/7.6 x 20.4cm strip. Create a wedge (see page 17) by folding the strip from one end to the other, secure the end, then lightly felt the entire surface.

2. Refine the shape into a right triangle, forming the first half of the grilled cheese sandwich.

CRUST

3. Thoroughly blend the Ocher and Chocolate. Take half of the blended wool and roll a strip of crust color between your palms. Felt the crust onto the two edges of the triangle that will represent the outer crust of the completed sandwich.

CHEESE

4. Thoroughly blend the Tangerine and Marigold and divide the mixture in half. Roll a strip of the blended wool between your palms and wrap it all the way around the edge of the triangle. Try to keep the strip in a straight line as you felt it into position in the center of the edge.

Tip

Try making pumpernickel swirled rye bread to make this project a bit fancier.

TOASTING

5. Take one tuft of Ocher and pull it apart slightly with your fingers. Lay the loose tuft onto the top of your sandwich and felt over the entire surface. Turn the sandwich over and repeat the toasting effect on the other side.

ILLUMINATE YOUR GRILLED CHEESE

6. Following the guidelines on page 22, use Lemon and Pale Yellow to add highlights to the cheese. Repeats Steps 1–6 to create the second half of the sandwich, as shown here. ■

Hot Dog

Here the bun is made in one solid piece, then cut down the center, which can be tricky. Don't worry if your cut is somewhat crooked or if the process seems difficult. This is a great chance to try "erasing" a mistake by felting over a spot if you feel you need to.

SUPPLIES

Basic tools (see pages 8–11)

INGREDIENTS

To make one hot dog

7 grams of a Pale Yellow and Buff blend (for the bun)

4 grams of an Ocher and Scarlet blend (for the hot dog)

1 gram of an Ocher and Chocolate blend (for the crust)

1 hearty tuft of Marigold (for the mustard)

1 tuft each of Ocher and Pale Yellow (for the bun highlights)

1 pinch of Pale Yellow (for the mustard highlights)

1 pinch each of Ocher, Pale Yellow, and Natural White (for the hot dog highlights)

BUN

1. Thoroughly blend the Pale Yellow and Buff. Lay out the blended wool in a 5 x 10"/12.7 x 25.4cm strip and roll it into a cylinder. Secure the ends and lightly felt the entire surface.

2. Flatten the sides, top, and bottom of the cylinder, forming a rectangle with rounded corners. Our bun is about 3"/7.6cm long by 1½"/3.8cm high.

3. Beginning about ½"/1.3cm up from the bottom of the bun, cut the rectangle lengthwise down the center.

HOT DOG

4. Thoroughly blend the Ocher and Scarlet. Lay out the blended wool in a 4 x 8"/10.2 x 20.4cm strip and roll it into a cylinder. Secure the end.

5. Place your hot dog into the bun and felt it into place. Continue to felt your hot dog to both shrink it down and further attach it to the bun.

BUN CRUST

6. Thoroughly blend the Ocher and Chocolate. Roll two strips of the blended wool between your palms. Wrap one around each side of your bun, extending all the way to the bottom.

Tip

Add more toppings.
There's always room
for ketchup and relish.

MUSTARD

7. Roll a strip of Marigold between your palms and
tack one end to the top of your hot dog. Use the tip of
the needle to "draw" curves with the Marigold as you
felt it down from one end of the hot dog to the other.

ILLUMINATE YOUR HOTDOG

8. Following the guidelines on page 22, use Ocher
and Pale Yellow to add highlights to the bun. Likewise,
use Ocher, Pale Yellow, and Natural White to add
highlights to the hot dog, and use Pale Yellow to add
highlights to the mustard. ■

Cheeseburger & Root Beer Float

Making the cheeseburger in one piece saves time and wool. You can get creative with your toppings if you're comfortable experimenting. When felting the float, make your pokes straight up and down rather than at an angle to avoid breaking your needle on the inside of the glass.

SUPPLIES

Basic tools (see pages 8–11)

Small float glass (available at a hobby store)

6"/15.2cm-long white pipe cleaner (for the straw)

E-6000 craft adhesive

Root Beer Float

INGREDIENTS

To make one classic root beer float

6 grams of Chocolate (for the root beer)

1 gram of Pelsull Ocher (for the melted ice cream)

5 grams of Natural White (for the scoop of vanilla ice cream)

1 gram each of Natural White and Red (for the straw)

 Note

Once your wool is firm, you can remove it from the glass, add a drop of E-6000 craft adhesive to the bottom of the glass, and then slip your wool back in. This will hold it in place.

ROOT BEER

1. Divide the Chocolate into thirds. Press the first third down into the glass and felt thoroughly. Be careful to work gently and not break your needle on the glass. (See Note.) Repeat with the other two thirds of the Chocolate.

MELTED ICE CREAM

2. Cover the top of the Chocolate with a layer of Pelsull Ocher, then felt the wool, focusing on the edges and smoothing out any gaps between layers.

53

VANILLA ICE CREAM

3. Reserve one-fifth of the Natural White to use in Step 4. Gather the remaining Natural White into a loose ball and press it into the top of the glass. Felt the ball into place, refining it into a dome shape. As in the previous step, carefully smooth out any gaps between the layers.

4. Using the Natural White reserved in Step 3, roll a strip between your palms. Wrap the strip around the base of the dome of the ice cream, just above the edge of the glass. Use the tip of your needle to gently form soft, random "ins and outs" as you felt the strip into place.

Try to create the look of a softly melted scoop of ice cream floating at the top of the glass.

STRAW

5. Fold the pipe cleaner in half. Take a pinch of Natural White and anchor it in the fold of the pipe cleaner. Twist the two lengths of the pipe cleaner together.

6. Roll a small amount of Natural White into a strip, then wrap it around the pipe cleaner. Gently felt the surface, taking care to avoid the wire as much as possible.

Tip

You can easily turn a float into a milkshake. Just fill the glass with any flavor and add whipped topping from the Pumpkin Pie.

See page 123

7. Roll a small strip of Red between your palms, tack one end of the strip to the top of the straw, then wrap the strip diagonally around the pipe cleaner, creating the illusion of a fountain straw. Felt the straw gently.

8. Cut a small hole in the top of your ice cream dome and insert your straw. Felt around the base of the straw to secure it in place. ■

Cheeseburger

INGREDIENTS

To make one cheeseburger

9 grams of a Pale Yellow and Ocher blend (for the bun)

1 gram of Chocolate (for the burger)

1 tuft of a Lemon Lime and Kiwi blend (for the lettuce)

1 tuft of a Marigold and Lemon blend (for the cheese)

1 tuft of Red (for the tomato)

1 tuft of Pale Yellow (for the bun highlights)

1 pinch each of Lemon and Pale Yellow (for the cheese highlights)

1 pinch each of Tangerine, Marigold, and Pale Yellow (for the tomato highlights)

Pinches of Natural White (for the seeds)

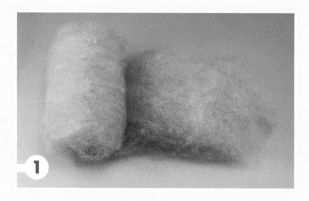

BUN

1. Thoroughly blend the Pale Yellow and Ocher. Lay out the blended wool in a 3 x 9"/7.6 x 22.9cm strip. Beginning at one end, roll up the wool into a cylinder and felt the end of the strip into place.

2. Continue to refine the shape by flattening one end of the cylinder and leaving the other end slightly rounded, like a bun.

Tip

Try adding a bit of purple wool to include a slice of red onion.

BURGER

3. Roll a strip of Chocolate approximately ½"/1.3cm wide between your palms. Wrap the strip around the center of your bun and felt it into place.

LETTUCE

4. Thoroughly blend the Lemon Lime and Kiwi. Roll a thin strip of the blended wool and felt one end of the strip into place, just below the burger. Use your needle to create uneven folds and wrinkles as you felt it into place. Think ruffled edges of lettuce.

CHEESE

5. Thoroughly blend the Marigold and Lemon. Roll four strips of the blended wool, each approximately 1"/2.5cm long. One at a time, carefully tack each strip to the side of the burger. Using the tip of your needle, carefully "pull" the center of each strip down to a point, forming an upside-down triangle that will mimic melted cheese.

Tip

The cheeseburger is a great option for our paperweight project.

See page 135

TOMATO

6. Divide the Red into 2 pinches and roll each slightly between your palms. Felt the tomato slices around your burger here and there, just above the cheese.

ILLUMINATE YOUR CHEESEBURGER; ADD SEEDS

7. Following the guidelines on page 22, use the tuft of Pale Yellow to highlight your bun before highlighting the rest of the cheeseburger. Use the Lemon and Pale Yellow to add highlights to the cheese. Use Tangerine, Marigold, and Pale Yellow to add highlights to the tomatoes. Last, take small pinches of Natural White, roll them between your fingers, and felt them to the top of the bun to mimic seeds. ∎

Cup o' Joe

We use a pipe cleaner to make the handle more stable. Remember that the center of a pipe cleaner is metal, so use extra care when felting this component. The incisions you'll cut into the side of the mug need to be just big enough to slip in the ends of your pipe cleaner.

SUPPLIES

Basic tools (see pages 8–11)

8"/20.4cm-long white pipe cleaner (for the cup handle)

INGREDIENTS

To make one cup o' joe

10 grams of a Taupe and Pale Yellow blend (for the cup)

1 gram of Chocolate (for the coffee)

2 tufts of Red (for the stripes on the cup)

1 pinch each of Ocher, Marigold, and Pale Yellow (for the coffee highlights)

1 pinch each of Natural White and Bright White (for the cup highlights)

1 pinch each of Tangerine, Marigold, and Pale Yellow (for the stripe highlights)

1 pinch of Scarlet (for the stripe shadows)

CUP

1. Thoroughly blend the Taupe and Pale Yellow, reserving 1 gram to be used in Step 6. Lay out the blended wool in a 3 x 12"/7.6 x 30.5cm strip, roll it into a cylinder, and secure the end.

2. As you refine the cylinder, create a slight hourglass shape by felting more intensely around the middle of the cup than around the top and bottom.

COFFEE

3. Form a small circle of Chocolate to represent the coffee. Felt the coffee on the top of the cup, leaving about ¼"/6.4mm around the edge.

STRIPES ON THE CUP

4. Roll two narrow strips of Red between your palms. Wrap them around the top of the cup. Leave a small space between the two stripes as you felt them into position.

CUP HANDLE

5. Fold the pipe cleaner in half, then twist the two lengths together.

6. Using the blended wool reserved from Step 1, wrap the pipe cleaner in the cup color, leaving ½"/1.3cm of the pipe cleaner exposed at each end. Felt the wool carefully onto the pipe cleaner.

7. Cut two small holes in the side of your cup, one slightly down from the top edge and one slightly up from the bottom. Make sure the two holes are properly aligned. Curve the pipe cleaner into a C shape and insert the exposed ends into the holes. Felt the handle carefully to the cup.

ILLUMINATE YOUR CUP O' JOE

8. Following the guidelines on page 22, use Ocher, Marigold, and Pale Yellow to add highlights to the coffee. Likewise, use Natural White and Bright White to add highlights to the cup, and use Tangerine, Marigold, and Pale Yellow to add highlights to the stripes. Use the Scarlet to add shadows to your stripes on the opposite side of your cup. ■

Farmers Market

FRESH PICKED

STRAWBERRY

PEACH HALF

AVOCADO HALF

WATERMELON WEDGE

CARROT

CUT LIME

APPLE HALF

Strawberry

Making the seeds for this project is time consuming, so be prepared to settle in when you're working on them—the end result is worth the extra effort!

SUPPLIES
Basic tools (see pages 8–11)

INGREDIENTS
To make one 2"/5.1cm-high strawberry

6 grams of a Red and Brick Red blend (for the main body)

1 gram of Tangerine (for the flesh midtones)

1 gram of a Tangerine and Pale Pink blend (for the lighter tones)

Pinches of Ocher and Marigold (for the seeds)

5 tufts of Kiwi (for the leaves and stem)

1 pinch each of Pale Yellow and Bright White (for the flesh highlights)

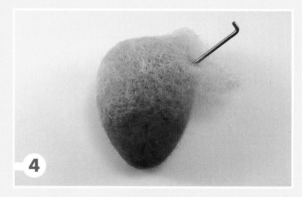

MAIN BODY

1. Thoroughly blend the Red and Brick Red. Gather the blended wool into a loose ball and lightly felt the surface.

2. Refine the shape by tapering one end of the ball to a slight point.

FLESH MIDTONES

3. Cover the top two-thirds of your strawberry shape with Tangerine. Felt over the whole surface, pulling off any uneven bits of Tangerine wool. Be careful not to make a straight line at the bottom where the colors shift.

FLESH LIGHTER TONES

4. Thoroughly blend the Tangerine and Pale Pink. Cover the top third of your strawberry with the blended wool. Felt over the whole surface, again pulling off any bits of wool that seem out of place and avoiding making a straight line at the bottom where the colors shift.

Tip

Dip your strawberries in chocolate by adding white or brown wool to the bottoms.

SEEDS

5. To make the seeds, first roll a small pinch of wool into a ball between your fingers, and then felt the seed into place on the surface of your strawberry. Use the tip of your needle to gently pull the top of each seed to a point as you felt it. Repeat the process as many times as needed. Use Ocher for the seeds at the bottom, and then change to Marigold about one-third from the bottom, making sure they're all evenly spaced.

LEAVES AND STEM

6. Form leaves for the strawberry using tufts of Kiwi, leaving the stem ends unfelted. Attach the loose ends of the leaves one at a time, then the stem, to the top of your strawberry.

ILLUMINATE YOUR STRAWBERRY

7. Following the guidelines on page 22, use Pale Yellow and Bright White to add highlights to your strawberry. ■

Peach Half

Using dark and light wool to accent our pit—darker wool in the grooves and lighter wool on the ridges—made it more three-dimensional. This is a great opportunity to practice illuminating a project, which will make your pieces look even more realistic.

SUPPLIES
Basic tools (see pages 8–11)

INGREDIENTS
To make one peach half

8 grams of a Tangerine and Marigold blend (for the main body)

1 tuft each of Tangerine and Scarlet (for the skin blush)

2 grams of Pelsull Ocher (for the pit)

1 tuft of Chocolate (for the pit ridges)

1 pinch each of Ocher and Pale Yellow (for the pit highlights)

1 tuft of Kiwi (for the leaf)

1 tuft of Scarlet (for the pit lining)

1 pinch each of Lemon, Pale Yellow, and Bright White (for the surface highlights)

1 pinch each of Lemon and Pale Yellow (for the skin highlights)

1 tuft of Ocher (for the surface edge outline)

MAIN BODY

1. Thoroughly blend the Tangerine and Marigold. Gather the blended wool into a loose sphere and felt it lightly.

2. Start to form your peach half by flattening one side of the sphere.

3. Continue to refine your peach half by tapering the bottom so it forms a slight point, then felt a deep groove into the top. As you work the rounded back of your peach half, leave a stripe about ¼"/6.4mm wide down the middle of the peach from the groove at the top to the point. Be careful not to felt this stripe too much, as you want it to form a slight ridge.

4. Add skin blush to the back of your peach using thin, wispy tufts of Tangerine and Scarlet.

PIT
5. Roll a loose ball of Pelsull Ocher and felt it into place in the center of the flat side to form the pit.

PIT RIDGES AND HIGHLIGHTS
6. Lay three thin strips of Chocolate lengthwise down the pit, then felt them carefully to form deep grooves. Following the guidelines on page 22, use Ocher and Pale Yellow to add highlights to the ridges between the grooves.

7

8

Tip

The beautiful natural color variations in a peach make this project perfect to experiment with a range of color and really practice blending.

LEAF AND PIT LINING

7. Felt a leaf shape with the Kiwi, leaving one end loose, then attach the loose end into the groove at the top of the peach. Roll a strip of Scarlet between your palms and use it to "draw" a felted line around the pit.

ILLUMINATE YOUR PEACH

8. Following the guidelines on page 22, use Lemon, Pale Yellow, and Bright White to add highlights to the cut side of your peach. Likewise, use Lemon and Pale Yellow to add highlights to the skin. Roll a thin strip of Ocher and use it to "draw" an outline around the very outer edge of the face of your peach. ■

Avocado Half

You can easily turn this project in a whole avocado. Just begin by making a second avocado half without the pit, cut a hole in the center, and lightly felt the surface of the hole with the color on the outer edge of the pit. The two pieces should fit together like a puzzle.

SUPPLIES
Basic tools (see pages 8–11)

INGREDIENTS
To make one avocado half

8 grams of Moss Green (for the main body)

2 grams of Pelsull Ocher (for the pit)

1 gram of Kiwi (for the surface)

1 tuft of a Lemon Lime and Kiwi blend (for the outer edge)

1 tuft of a Pale Yellow and Lemon Lime blend (for the pit lining)

1 pinch each of Ocher, Marigold, and Pale Yellow (for the pit highlight)

MAIN BODY

1. Reserving a tuft to be used in Step 7, gather the Moss Green into a rough oval shape and begin to felt the surface lightly.

2. Continue to felt the wool to refine your avocado shape by tapering one end slightly. Felt one side flat to make the cut side of your avocado.

PIT

3. Roll the Pelsull Ocher to form a rough oval shape that's slightly smaller than the flat surface of the avocado. Tack the pit onto the flat side, then continue to shape it.

SURFACE

4. Cover the flat surface around the pit with the Kiwi.

OUTER EDGE

5. Thoroughly blend the Lemon Lime and Kiwi. Roll a thin strip of the blended wool between your palms. Carefully outline the surface color as you tack the outer edge into place.

PIT LINING

6. Thoroughly blend the Pale Yellow and Lemon Lime. Roll a strip of the blended wool and use it to outline the pit.

Tip

The avocados make fresh ornaments. Try our ornament project in Serving Suggestions.

See page 140

REFINING THE CUT EDGE

7. Wrap the reserved tuft of Moss Green around the top edge of your fruit to hide the seam between the Kiwi and the avocado body.

ILLUMINATE YOUR AVOCADO

8. Following the guidelines on page 22, use Ocher, Marigold, and Pale Yellow to add highlights to the avocado pit. ∎

Watermelon Wedge

Crafting a watermelon wedge is a fun way to practice details. From the highlights on the seeds to the stripes on the rind, this projects offers plenty of opportunities to use your shading and shaping skills to make your watermelon look like it was just picked off the vine.

SUPPLIES
Basic tools (see pages 8–11)

INGREDIENTS
To make one watermelon wedge

7 grams of a Rose and Marigold blend (for the flesh)

1 gram of a Pale Pink and Pale Yellow blend (for the pale inner rind)

1 gram of a Kiwi and Moss Green blend (for the outer rind)

1 tuft of a Lemon Lime and Pale Yellow blend (for the inner rind)

1 tuft each of Espresso and Pale Yellow (for the seeds)

1 pinch each of Ocher and Pale Yellow (for the seed highlights)

1 pinch each of Tangerine and Marigold (for the flesh highlights)

MAIN BODY

1. Thoroughly blend the Rose and Marigold. Lay out the blended wool in a 5 x 10"/12.7 x 25.4cm strip and felt lightly over the whole surface.

2. Create a wedge (see page 17) by folding the strip onto itself from one end to the other, then securing the end.

3. Transform the triangle into a wedge by flattening the sides and top as you felt the wedge.

WHITE INNER RIND

4. Thoroughly blend the Pale Pink and Pale Yellow. Cover the top third of the wedge (both sides) with the blended wool, and then felt the whole surface.

OUTER RIND

5. Lightly blend the Kiwi and Moss Green, being careful not to mix these colors too much, as the outer rind should have a kind of striped look. Cover the top of the watermelon wedge with the mixture. Felt over the whole top edge, neatening up the loose edges as you work.

CUT EDGE OF THE RIND

6. Thoroughly blend the Lemon Lime and Pale Yellow. Roll a strip of the blended wool between your palms. Wrap it around the wedge at the very top, just below the edge of the outer rind, and then felt the strip of wool flat.

7

8

SEEDS

7. Roll small balls of Espresso between your fingertips. Then felt them onto the surface of the watermelon, using the tip of your needle to form the balls into seed shapes as you work. Repeat the process with Pale Yellow to form the watermelon's white seeds.

ILLUMINATE YOUR WATERMELON

8. Add highlights to the brown seeds using Ocher and Pale Yellow. Following the guidelines on page 22, use Tangerine and Marigold to add highlights to the edge of the watermelon flesh. ■

VARIATION

To make a watermelon slice, transform the triangle in Step 2 into a half-circle by rounding the L-shaped sides.

Carrot

The world of carrots is a colorful one, so don't feel you need to limit yourself to just orange. Beautiful carrots are out there in a variety of colors. Go wild with purple, red, and yellow carrots—and maybe even consider needle felting a parsnip or two to add to your beautiful bunch.

SUPPLIES
Basic tools (see pages 8–11)

8"/20.3cm-long pipe cleaner (for the stem)

INGREDIENTS
To make one carrot

6 grams of a Tangerine and Marigold blend (for the main body)

4 tufts of Marigold (for the stripes)

1 gram of Kiwi (for the stem)

1 pinch of Pale Yellow (for the highlights)

MAIN BODY

1. Thoroughly blend the Tangerine and Marigold. Lay out the blended wool in a strip approximately 5 x 8"/12.7 x 20.3cm. Fold over the top 1"/2.5cm.

2. Beginning at one end, roll the strip into a tight cylinder. Be sure to keep the folded edge on the inside. Secure the end and lightly felt the entire surface.

3. Transform the cylinder into a tapered cone, rounding the thicker end slightly and working the narrower end into a point.

STRIPES
4. Using Marigold, add stripes of varying thicknesses around the body of your carrot. Cover the carrot's tip as well, twisting any extra Marigold between your fingers to form the carrot's root.

5. Felt deep grooves around your carrot just above each stripe of Marigold.

STEM
6. Place a small pinch of Kiwi at the midway point of a pipe cleaner. Fold the pipe cleaner in half so it sandwiches the wool, then twist the two lengths of the pipe cleaner together, stopping when you get three-quarters of the way down.

Tip

Make mini carrots and add them to the Easter Bunny Centerpiece.

See page 138

7. Insert a second small pinch of Kiwi between the two lengths of pipe cleaner and finish twisting them together. Divide the remaining Kiwi into two halves. Use the first half to roll a ½"/1.3cm strip between your palms. Wrap the strip tightly around the folded pipe cleaner. Felt the strip gently into place, being careful to avoid hitting the wire as much as possible.

8. Roll the second half of Kiwi between your palms to form another ½"/1.3cm strip. Tack one end of the strip into place near the top of the pipe cleaner, then wrap the rest around the stem, using the tip of your needle to create loops and felting them into place as you go.

ILLUMINATE YOUR CARROT

9. Cut a small hole in the top of your carrot about 1"/2.5cm deep. Insert the stem into the hole and felt it gently into place (again, taking care to avoid the wire). Following the guidelines on page 22, add highlights to your carrot using Pale Yellow. ■

Cut Lime

When you're comfortable taking chances with your needle felting, you can use the basic elements of this project to turn a lime into a grapefruit or an orange. You can even just swap out our colors to make a lemon. Simply adjust the shape to the fruit you desire, change the colors, and *bam*—you've made a fresh fruit stand!

SUPPLIES
Basic tools (see pages 8–11)

INGREDIENTS
To make one cut lime

9 grams of a Kiwi and Moss Green blend (for the main body)

1 gram of Kiwi (for the flesh)

3 tufts of Pale Yellow (for the segments)

1 tuft of Natural White (for the pith)

1 pinch each of Kiwi, Lemon, and Pale Yellow (for the peel highlights)

1 pinch each of Lemon and Pale Yellow (for the flesh highlights)

MAIN BODY

1. Thoroughly blend the Kiwi and Moss Green. Form the blended wool into a loose ball and lightly felt the surface.

2. Continue to refine the shape by tapering the ends of the ball, leaving a small bump on each end.

3. Once your lime feels dense or solid enough, use scissors to cut a wedge out of it.

FLESH

4. Cover the cut surface with Kiwi, leaving about ¼"/6.4mm all the way around the edge for the peel.

SEGMENTS

5. Roll three thin strips of Pale Yellow between your palms. Use one to form a V whose point sits in the center of the cut's crease and felt into place, then repeat on the opposite side. Felt the third strip into the crease's center.

PITH

6. Roll a strip of Natural White between your palms and use it to outline the cut edges of the lime.

ILLUMINATE YOUR LIME

7. Use Kiwi, Lemon, and Pale Yellow to add highlights to the peel and Lemon and Pale Yellow to add highlights to the flesh. ■

Apple Half

Don't limit your apple selection to red, or any one color for that matter—a whole orchard of colorful apples awaits! Mix it up by adding some bright green Granny Smiths or colorful Ginger Golds to your needle-felted fruit bowl.

SUPPLIES

Basic tools (see pages 8–11)

INGREDIENTS

To make one apple half

8 grams of a Red and Brick Red blend (for the main body)

1 gram of a Pale Yellow and Natural White blend (for the flesh)

1 tuft of Ocher (for the seam)

2 tufts of Chocolate (for the seeds)

1 tuft of Kiwi (for the leaf)

1 pinch each of Tangerine and Marigold and Natural White (for the apple skin highlights)

1 pinch each of Ocher and Natural White (for the seed highlights)

MAIN BODY

1. Thoroughly blend the Red and Brick Red. Gather the blended wool into a ball and felt it into a sphere.

2. Continue to refine the shape, tapering the sphere slightly to form the base of the apple.

3. Work one side of the apple until it is flat. Felt a deep groove in the center of the top of the apple, where the leaf will sit.

FLESH

4. Thoroughly blend the Pale Yellow and Natural White. Cover the flat part of the apple with the blended wool and felt it into position. Carefully work around the edges to make a neat circle.

SEAM AND SEEDS

5. Roll a small thread of Ocher to indicate the seam. Lay it down in the center of the apple flesh and felt it into position. Using Chocolate, roll two small ovals for the seeds. Felt them into place, forming the tops of the ovals into little points as you work.

LEAF

6. Fold the Kiwi into a rough leaf shape. Felt the top of the leaf to create your desired shape, but be careful to leave the bottom of the leaf unfelted so you can attach it to the apple. Tack the loose end of the leaf into the groove at the top of the apple.

ILLUMINATE YOUR APPLE

7. Following the guidelines on page 22, use Tangerine and Marigold to add highlights to the apple skin. Use Natural White to add highlights to the seeds. ■

VARIATION

To make a whole apple, simply skip steps 3–5 and finish by illuminating the apple's skin.

Sweet Shop

DELECTABLE DESSERTS

VANILLA ICE CREAM CONE

CHOCOLATE CHIP COOKIE

FROSTED LAYER CAKE

FROSTED CUPCAKE

CHOCOLATE-COVERED
DOUGHNUT

MACARON

CHERRY PIE SLICE

Vanilla Ice Cream Cone

The cone makes this project really stand out—the texture details elevate this project to nothing short of amazing. This is also an easy project to customize by changing the flavor of ice cream. Fancy mint chocolate chip? Just use Lemon Lime for the ice cream and Espresso for the chocolate chunks.

SUPPLIES
Basic tools (see pages 8–11)

INGREDIENTS
To make one vanilla ice cream cone

7 grams of an Ocher and Chocolate blend (for the cone)

1 gram of Ocher (for the ridges)

7 grams of Natural White (for the vanilla ice cream)

CONE

1. Thoroughly blend the Ocher and Chocolate. Lay out the blended wool in a 5 x 10"/12.7 x 25.4cm strip.

2. Fold the bottom left corner of the strip up to meet the top edge.

3. Fold the bottom right corner of the strip over to meet the left edge. Felt the wool into place.

4. Continue to refine the shape by flattening the top of the cone and smoothing out the sides.

RIDGES

5. One at a time, roll eight strips of Ocher between your palms. Starting with the first strip, attach one end at the top edge of the cone and wrap it around the cone at a diagonal angle toward the bottom, then felt it into place. Repeat this process in the same direction with three more strips. Then add the four remaining strips in the opposite diagonal direction, being mindful of how the strips cross each other.

VANILLA ICE CREAM

6. To make the vanilla ice cream, form the Natural White into a loose ball by gathering all the ends together and holding them in one hand. Felt one side of the balled wool into a half-sphere, leaving the ends in your hand loose.

7. Once the half-sphere holds its shape well, "open" the loose ends by pulling them out to the sides. Place the half-sphere onto the top of the cone and felt it into place by working around the top of your cone, still leaving the ends loose.

8. Roll the loose ends in toward your cone and use the tip of your needle to create interesting shapes in the wool as you felt the roll into place. ■

Chocolate Chip Cookie

This is a great project for novice needle felters, and a great place to start when teaching children the wonders of needle felting. Once you've made your basic shape, the sky's the limit with how you can decorate your cookie. We've given you three examples to get you started.

SUPPLIES
Basic tools (see pages 8–11)

INGREDIENTS
To make one chocolate chip cookie

5 grams of a Pale Yellow and Ocher blend (for the cookie)

1 gram of Pelsull Ocher (for the browned cookie bottom)

1 tuft of an Ocher and Pale Yellow blend (for the cookie highlights)

Tufts of Chocolate (as needed) (for the chocolate chips)

1 pinch each of Ocher and Natural White (for the highlights on the chocolate chips)

MAIN BODY

1. Thoroughly blend the Pale Yellow and Ocher. Roll the blended wool into a loose ball and felt it gently.

2. Continue to refine the ball, transforming it into a disk as you work. Flatten one side completely and leave the other side slightly domed.

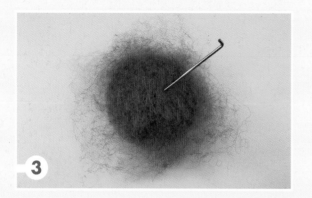

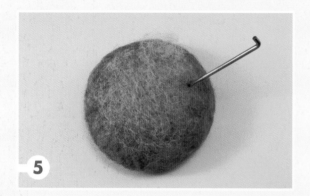

BROWNED COOKIE BOTTOM

3. Cover the flat side of your cookie in a thin layer of Pelsull Ocher, leaving about ¼"/6.4mm of loose wool around the edge. Felt the whole surface.

4. Flip your cookie over and pull the loose Pelsull Ocher up around the edge, then felt it flat.

COOKIE HIGHLIGHTS

5. Thoroughly blend the Ocher and Pale Yellow. Position the blended wool in the center of the dome of your cookie, then felt it flat.

CHOCOLATE CHIPS

6. Using a pinch of Chocolate, roll a ball between your fingertips and felt it into place. Repeat the process. Make as many chips as you please, varying the size of each slightly.

7. Following the guidelines on page 22, use Ocher and Natural White to add highlights to your chocolate chips. ▪

VARIATIONS

To make a black-and-white cookie, follow Steps 1 and 2. Next, cover half of the domed surface with Natural White. Felt the wool into place, making a straight line down the center and leaving a ¹⁄₁₆"/1.6mm border around the edge. Cover the remaining half of the domed surface with Chocolate, matching the straight line in the center, and again leaving a ¹⁄₁₆"/1.6mm border around the edge. Add highlights to the chocolate half using Ocher and Pale Yellow.

To make an iced sugar cookie, follow Steps 1 and 2, then use your choice of colors to decorate your cookie. We used pink icing with red icing in the center.

Frosted Cake Slice

We don't use core wool (see page 7) in this food, but if you wanted to experiment it's a good one to try it out on. Simply felt your cylinder shape out of core wool, then wrap it in the colors you choose for your cake and frosting. Be sure to cover all of the core wool with colorful wool.

SUPPLIES
Basic tools (see pages 8–11)

INGREDIENTS
To make one slice of frosted cake

12 grams of a Pale Yellow and Ocher blend (for the vanilla cake)

4 grams of Chocolate (for the chocolate frosting)

1 pinch each of Ocher and Pale Yellow (for the chocolate frosting highlights)

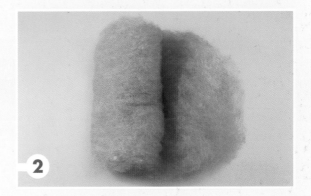

CAKE

1. Thoroughly blend the Pale Yellow and Ocher. Lay out the blended wool in a strip approximately 5 x 12"/12.7 x 30.5cm.

2. Beginning at one end, roll up the strip into a loose cylinder. Secure the ends and lightly felt the entire surface.

3. Transform the shape into a wedge by felting the right edge of the cylinder into a point. Work the left edge from the side to create a flat plane, then flatten the top and bottom of the wedge.

FROSTING; ILLUMINATE YOUR FROSTING

4. Roll 1 gram of Chocolate wool into a strip ½"/1.3cm wide. Starting at the middle of the back of the wedge and working all the way around, felt the strip down the center.

5. Cover the back and top of the wedge with 2 grams of Chocolate, working the wool until the edges of the frosting line up correctly with the edges of the cake.

6. Take your remaining gram of Chocolate and roll two strips, each about ½"/1.3cm wide. Lay one across the top of the back edge and one along the bottom. Create "ins and outs" along the two strips as you felt them into place.

7. Following the guidelines on page 22, use Ocher and Pale Yellow to add highlights to the frosting. ■

Frosted Cupcake

The wrapper is what makes this cupcake so special. The secret is to keep your wool loose when working on the bottom of the wrapper. Begin with a little wool and add more if you want a more opaque look. Here's another chance to make a project your own.

SUPPLIES

Basic tools (see pages 8–11)

INGREDIENTS

To make one frosted red velvet cupcake

12 grams of Scarlet (for the cake)

1 gram of a Brick Red and Buff blend (for the wrapper)

4 grams of Natural White (for the buttercream frosting)

CUPCAKE

1. Begin by forming a loose ball with the Scarlet.

2. Refine the shape by flattening the bottom of the ball and straightening the sides, leaving the top slightly domed.

WRAPPER

3. Thoroughly blend the Brick Red and Buff. Divide your blended wool into several pieces, each 1"/2.5cm to 2"/5cm long. Lay them side by side in a line on your pad until you have one 9"/22.9cm-long strip. Use any remaining blended wool to roll a 9"/22.9cm-long piece between your palms and lay it along the top edge of the row of tufts. Lightly felt the top half of the strip, leaving the bottom edge loose.

4. Tack one end of the tufted strip into place on the cupcake body about one-quarter of the way down from the top with the finished edge up. Wrap the tufted strip around the cupcake and felt it into place.

5. Continue to smooth out the wrapper as you felt it onto the cupcake body. As you work, make sure to pull off any small tufts that make it look uneven.

6. Felt sixteen deep grooves all the way around the wrapper. To get them as even as possible, it's helpful to mark where they will go by looking at the bottom of your cupcake. Think of the bottom as a compass and begin by felting grooves at the North, South, East, and West points. Then felt grooves down the middle of each of those four sections. Finally, divide those eight sections in half again.

BUTTERCREAM FROSTING

7. Form a loose ball of Natural White. Hold the ball in one hand, pinching one side into a point with your finger and thumb. Working with the other hand, carefully felt the wool, transforming the ball into a gentle cone shape.

8. Tack the frosting onto the top of your cupcake. Starting at the bottom edge, felt a deep spiral into your cone up toward the center. This will help sculpt your icing, refine the cone shape, and further secure it to the base of the cupcake. ◼

Chocolate-Covered Doughnut

This is a great project to tailor to the doughnut lover in your life. It's easy to add sprinkles, cream filling, or other flavors of frosting just by switching up your color blends and adding details that can make each doughnut a special creation invented by you.

SUPPLIES

Basic tools (see pages 8–11)

12"/30.5cm pipe cleaner (for the doughnut frame)

INGREDIENTS

To make one chocolate-covered doughnut

7 grams of a Pale Yellow and Ocher blend (for the main body)

1 tuft of Pale Yellow (for the edge)

1 gram of Chocolate (for the chocolate frosting)

1 pinch each of Ocher and Pale Yellow (for the chocolate frosting highlights)

Note

To help give the pipe cleaner that forms the doughnut a round shape, you can wrap it around a bottle or jar that's about 3"/7.6cm in diameter.

MAIN BODY

1. Thoroughly blend the Pale Yellow and Ocher. Form the pipe cleaner into a circle, twisting the ends around each other and sandwiching a few small tufts of wool between them to anchor them together as you twist. Divide the remaining wool into thirds.

2. Take a third of the wool and form a long strip, rolling it gently between your palms. Wrap the strip around the circle and felt it carefully into place.

3. Use another third of the wool to wrap the circle again, then felt over the whole surface.

4. Use the final third of wool to smooth out the top and bottom and to cover any of the wrapping marks.

EDGE

5. Roll a strip of Pale Yellow between your palms and wrap it around the center of the outer edge of your doughnut. Felt the wool carefully into place.

FROSTING; ILLUMINATE YOUR FROSTING

6. Roll a strip of Chocolate between your palms and cover the top of your doughnut. Use the tip of your needle to create "drips" along the outside edge of your frosting, keeping the inside edge more of a perfect circle.

7. Following the guidelines on page 22, use Ocher and Pale Yellow to add highlights to your frosting. ■

Macaron

An assortment of colorful felt macarons, arranged lovingly in a box with pretty tissue paper, will make a delightful gift for the Francophile in your life. The lovely pastels are a delight to the eye, and this project looks good both with and without Kerri's special illumination technique (see page 22).

SUPPLIES

Basic tools (see pages 8–11)

INGREDIENTS

To make one pistachio macaron

6 grams of a Lemon, Kiwi, and Pale Yellow blend (for the main body)

1 gram of Pale Yellow (for the cream)

1 pinch each of Lemon and Pale Yellow (for the highlights)

2. Refine the shape by flattening the sides of the ball, leaving the top and bottom slightly domed.

CREAM

3. Roll a strip of Pale Yellow between your palms and wrap it around the center of your macaron. Felt the cream into place.

4. Roll each tuft of blended wool that you reserved in Step 1 between your palms to create two long strips. Wrap each strip around your macaron, one above and one below the cream.

ILLUMINATE YOUR MACARON

5. Following the guidelines on page 22, use Lemon and Pale Yellow to add highlights to the macaron. ■

MAIN BODY

1. Thoroughly blend the Lemon, Kiwi, and Pale Yellow, then reserve 2 tufts to use in Step 4. Form a loose ball with the remaining blended wool and gently felt it.

Cherry Pie Slice

Feeling blue? It's just as easy to make a blueberry or even a mixed-berry pie. The trick is the illumination technique (see page 22). To make your berries burst with light, place the felted pie under a lamp, notice where the natural highlights fall, then add them to your piece.

SUPPLIES
Basic tools (see pages 8–11)

INGREDIENTS
To make one slice of cherry pie

10 grams of a Brick Red and Scarlet blend (for the pie filling)

6 grams of a Pale Yellow and Ocher blend (for the crust)

2 grams of Red (for the cherries)

Pinches of Tangerine, Marigold, and Pale Yellow (for the cherry highlights)

PIE FILLING

1. Thoroughly blend the Brick Red and Scarlet. Lay out the blended wool into a strip approximately 5 x 10"/12.7 x 25.4cm.

2. Beginning at the bottom left corner and working to the right, triangle-fold (see page 17) the entire strip, then secure the end and lightly felt the surface.

CRUST

3. Continue to felt the wool for the filling, transforming the resulting triangle into a symmetrical wedge. Thoroughly blend Pale Yellow and Ocher. Lay out 4 grams of the blended wool in a triangle slightly larger than the wedge. (Set aside the remaining 2 grams of this blend to use in Step 6.) Felt over the entire triangle, flattening the surface.

4. Lay the crust wedge on top of the filling wedge, matching up the two tips. Flip both pieces over and fasten them together by felting over the whole surface. Work the edges of the crust until they line up with the edges of the wedge, leaving the back edge of the crust loose.

5. Roll the loose wool at the back edge of the crust down toward the front of the filling wedge and felt it into place. Create the look of crimped crust by felting deep grooves into the roll.

6. Using the blended wool reserved from Step 3, roll strips in varying lengths about ¾"/1.9cm wide, depending on the size of your wedge. These strips will be used to create the lattice on the top of your pie. Felt the strips one at a time, starting with the diagonals that go in one direction, then crossing the strips with opposing diagonals.

CHERRIES

7. Take tufts of Red in varying sizes and roll each into a ball between the palms of your hands. Felt each cherry into a random spot on your pie.

ILLUMINATE YOUR CHERRY PIE

8. Following the guidelines on page 22, use Tangerine, Marigold, and Pale Yellow to add highlights to your cherries. ◼

Holiday Treats

FESTIVE FAVORITES

VALENTINE'S LOLLIPOP

DARK CHOCOLATE BUNNY

ROCKET POP

CANDY CORN

PUMPKIN PIE SLICE

ICED GINGERBREAD MAN

Valentine's Lollipop

A trick of the trade when rolling wool between your palms, as you'll do in this project, is to lightly moisten your hands before you begin rolling. This will help the fibers bind together more easily and will give you a tighter roll to work with. Also, the lollipop is a thin piece, so be careful to use shallow pokes when adding your stripes to keep your colors from poking through.

SUPPLIES

Basic tools (see pages 8–11)

Lollipop stick

E-6000 craft adhesive

5"/12.7cm red curling ribbon (to decorate the stick)

INGREDIENTS

To make one heart lollipop

7 grams of Dusty Rose (for the main body)

1 gram of Brick Red (for the red swirls)

1 tuft of Buff (for the white swirls)

1 pinch each of Tangerine, Marigold, and Natural White (for the highlights on the red swirls)

Pinches of Pale Pink and Natural White (for the highlights on the pink swirls)

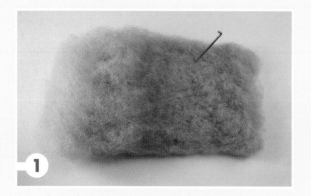

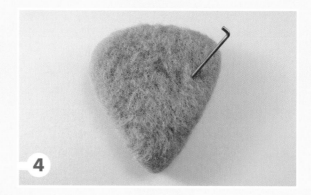

MAIN BODY

1. Lay out the Dusty Rose in a 4 x 8"/10.2 x 20.3cm strip (reserving a tuft to use in Step 9) and felt over the entire surface.

2. Fold the bottom left corner of the wool up to meet the top edge.

3. Fold the bottom right corner over to the left edge to form a triangle. Felt the entire surface.

4. Continue to refine the shape by rounding the top two corners of the triangle so they start to look like curves.

5. Felt a deep groove in the center of the top of the triangle so your shape starts to resemble a heart. Continue to define the top two curves.

6. Felt a deep, spiral-shaped groove in the center of the lollipop, beginning at the bottom edge and working toward the center. Try to keep an equal distance between the adjacent parts of the spiral groove. Repeat the spiral groove on the back side, using any visible pokes from your front spiral for guidance.

RED AND WHITE SWIRLS

7. Pinch off small tufts of Brick Red and felt them in place, creating swirls. Repeat the process with Buff to

5

6

7

8

create two thin white swirls that outline each thick red swirl. Repeat the swirls on the back side.

ILLUMINATE YOUR LOLLIPOP

8. Following the guidelines on page 22, use Tangerine, Marigold, and Natural White to add highlights to the red swirls. Likewise, use Pale Pink and Natural White to add highlights to the pink swirls. Repeat the highlights on the back side.

STICK

9. Put a small dab of E-6000 craft adhesive on the end of the lollipop stick and wrap it with the tuft of Dusty Rose reserved from Step 1. Cut a small hole in the

9

bottom of your lollipop, insert the stick, and carefully felt it into place. Then adorn the stick with a ribbon tied in a small bow. ■

Dark Chocolate Bunny

We love this sweet and simple idea! Using a cookie cutter to create these adorable bunnies makes it an ideal project for children to try. Any bunny-shaped cookie cutter you like will do, and you'll have total freedom in deciding what details to add.

SUPPLIES
Basic tools (see pages 8–11)

Cookie cutter in your favorite chocolate bunny shape

INGREDIENTS
To make one dark chocolate bunny

16 grams of Chocolate (for the main body)

1 gram of Ocher (for the midtones)

1 pinch each of Ocher, Pale Yellow, and Natural White (for the highlights)

Note

The cookie cutter we used is 6"/15.2cm tall by 3½"/8.9cm wide, and the wool amounts listed above worked for those dimensions. However, the quantities of wool you'll need will depend on the size of the cookie cutter you choose.

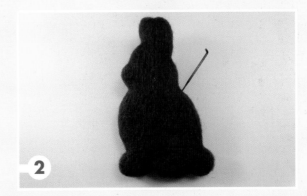

MAIN BODY

1. Fill your cookie cutter with Chocolate, pressing the wool all the way into the ears and other tight spots. When the cutter is filled to the top, felt the wool flat, then add more. Repeat until your bunny is firm and about ¾"/1.9cm thick.

2. Remove your bunny from the cutter and clean up its edges, using small pinches of wool to fill in any seams that may have formed between the layers.

115

Tip

Change the colors to make a milk or white chocolate bunny.

3. "Draw" lines on your bunny by felting deep grooves in its surface to define its legs, ears, and face.

MIDTONES

4. Following the guidelines on page 22, use thin layers of Ocher to define your bunny's midtones. These will make your bunny appear three-dimensional. Remember to apply the midtones so they create the appearance that a light source is illuminating the form from one direction only.

ILLUMINATE YOUR BUNNY

5. Using Ocher, Pale Yellow, and Natural White, add highlights to the bunny. ■

Rocket Pop

This is a really simple project because you're working with just one basic shape, the cylinder. Once that's ready to go, layering the colored wool on top is a snap. The rocket pop looks even more realistic through its clever use of a real popsicle stick, which you can find at your local craft supply store.

SUPPLIES

Basic tools (see pages 8–11)

Small popsicle stick

E-6000 craft adhesive

INGREDIENTS

To make one rocket pop

10 grams of Natural White (for the main body)

1 gram of Caribbean Sea (for the blue raspberry layer)

1 gram of Red (for the cherry layer)

1 additional gram of Natural White (for the lemon layer)

1 pinch each of Tangerine, Marigold, and Pale Yellow (for the cherry layer highlights)

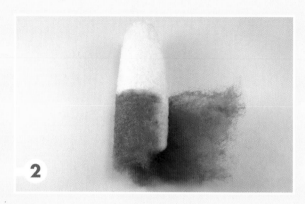

MAIN BODY

1. Lay out the Natural White in a 4 x 8"/10.2 x 20.3cm strip, reserving a tuft to use in Step 6. Beginning at one end, roll the strip into a cylinder and secure the end. Refine the shape of the pop by tapering one end into a rounded point and flattening the other end.

BLUE RASPBERRY LAYER

2. Wrap the bottom third of your rocket pop, including the flattened bottom, in Caribbean Sea. Felt the wool until it's flat.

CHERRY LAYER

3. Wrap the top third of the rocket pop in Red, then felt the wool until it's flat.

LEMON LAYER

4. Wrap the center third of the rocket pop in Natural White and felt the wool until it's flat.

Tip

Skip the ridges and use one color to make your favorite flavor in a traditional shape.

5. Felt eight deep grooves down the sides of your pop. The easiest way to space them evenly is to think about the bottom of the pop as if it were a compass. First, felt grooves at the North, South, East, and West points, then felt grooves down the middle of each of those four sections.

POPSICLE STICK

6. Place a dab of E-6000 craft adhesive on both sides of one end of a small popsicle stick, then wrap it with a tuft of Natural White. Cut a small hole in the center of the bottom of the pop and insert the wooly end of the popsicle stick into the hole. Carefully felt the stick in place.

ILLUMINATE YOUR ROCKET POP

7. Following the guidelines on page 22, use Tangerine, Marigold, and Pale Yellow to add highlights to the cherry layer of your rocket pop. ∎

Candy Corn

This is a great project for a beginner because it allows you to practice simple shaping skills while working with different colors. The candy corns' small size makes it tricky to avoid poking your fingers, so be extra safety-conscious while making these tiny treats.

SUPPLIES
Basic tools (see pages 8–11)

INGREDIENTS
To make one kernel of candy corn

1 gram of Natural White
(for the body)

1 pinch each of Tangerine and
Lemon (for the colors)

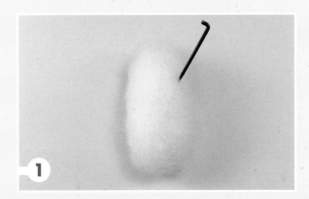

MAIN BODY

1. Set aside a pinch of Natural White to use in Step 5, then felt the rest into a small cylinder.

2. Round the corners of the cylinder at its top and bottom. Continue to refine the shape by felting the cylinder into a rounded triangle. Finish by flattening the top of the piece (the wide end of the triangle).

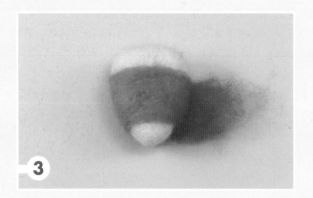

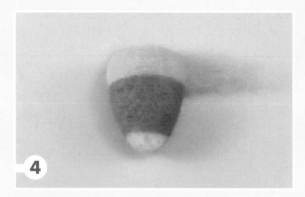

Tip

String a bunch of candy corn together to make a sweet garland.

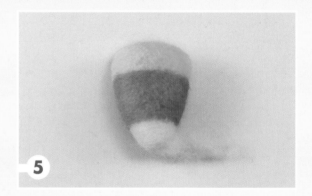

ADDING COLORS

3. When the shape is satisfactory, wrap its center with a pinch of Tangerine and felt it in place.

4. Wrap the top (the wide end) of the shape with Lemon and felt into place.

5. Finish the candy corn by wrapping its point with the pinch of Natural White reserved from Step 1 and felting it into place. ■

Pumpkin Pie Slice

We love the dollop of whipped cream in this project. You can use the recipe for the whipped cream in other projects too—just use your imagination. Also, you can easily turn pumpkin pie into a summery key lime pie by substituting the Tangerine and Ocher blend with a mix of Pale Yellow and Lemon Lime.

SUPPLIES

Basic tools (see pages 8–11)

INGREDIENTS

To make one slice of pumpkin pie

10 grams of a Tangerine and Ocher blend (for the pumpkin filling)

4 grams of a Pale Yellow and Ocher blend (for the crust)

3 grams of Natural White (for the whipped cream)

1 pinch each of Tangerine and Marigold (for the filling highlights)

123

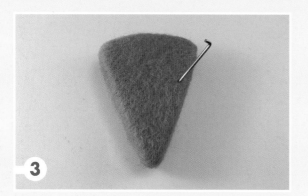

PUMPKIN FILLING

1. Thoroughly blend the Tangerine and Ocher. Lay out the blended wool in a 5 x 10"/12.7 x 25.4cm strip.

2. Starting at the bottom left corner, triangle-fold the wool (see page 17) until you reach the end of the strip, then secure the end and lightly felt the entire surface.

3. Refine the form by flattening the sides of the triangle and creating a wedge shape that resembles pie filling.

CRUST

4. Thoroughly blend the Pale Yellow and Ocher. Lay out the blended wool in a triangle that's slightly larger than the pie filling wedge and felt over the whole surface. Neaten the two side edges of the triangle as you work, but leave the top edge loose.

5. Place the pie filling on top of the crust, matching up the two tips. Flip both pieces over and fasten them to one another by felting from the bottom of the crust up into the pie filling. Wrap the top edge of the crust around the back of the pie filling wedge and felt the crust into place.

6. Roll the loose ends of the crust down toward the top of the pie filling and felt into place. Felt deep grooves in the roll to create a decorative edge.

WHIPPED CREAM

7. Roll the Natural White into a rough sphere. Pinch one side of your sphere and carefully felt the part of the sphere that is exposed as you hold the wool. Continue felting until the loose sphere maintains its shape, then felt the pinched side into a point to resemble a dollop of whipped cream.

ADD THE WHIPPED CREAM; ILLUMINATE YOUR PUMPKIN PIE

8. Felt the whipped cream to the top of your pumpkin pie. Starting at the bottom edge of the dollop and working up toward the center, felt a deep spiral into your whipped cream. Following the guidelines on page 22, use Tangerine and Marigold to add highlights to your pumpkin pie. ∎

Iced Gingerbread Man

Gingerbread people are fun to create. You can make a bunch of blank gingerbread people and let the kids in your life glue on decorations. This project is made in a cookie cutter, which offers an excellent opportunity to teach an older child about needle felting.

SUPPLIES

Basic tools (see pages 8–11)

Gingerbread man–shaped cookie cutter

INGREDIENTS

To make one gingerbread man (see Note below)

7 grams of Pelsull Ocher (for the cookie)

1 gram of Natural White (for the icing)

Note

The cookie cutter we used was 4"/10.2cm tall by 3"/7.6cm wide, so the wool amounts listed above suited our needs. However, the quantities of the ingredients that you'll need will depend on the size of the cookie cutter you choose. Also, there's no reason why this needs to be a gingerbread *man*; gingerbread women are equally appealing.

COOKIE

1. Fill your cutter with Pelsull Ocher, pressing the wool all the way into each of the extremities. Felt the wool until it's flat, then add another layer. Repeat until your cutter is full and your gingerbread man is firm.

2. Remove your gingerbread man from the cutter and clean up the edges. Use additional Pelsull Ocher to fill in any gaps between the layers.

Tip

Any cookie cutter will do for this project—felt all of your family's favorites.

ICING

3. Roll the Natural White between your palms, creating a long, thin strip. Carefully outline your gingerbread man, making sure to keep a small bit of brown visible along the edge.

4. Using the icing strip created in Step 3, add features to your gingerbread man—eyes, a smile, buttons, maybe even a bow tie. ■

Serving Suggestions

Ideas & Instructions for Wearing & Displaying Your Felted Food

Wear It!

PENDANTS

It's very easy to turn any of the foods into a pendant. You can make a food smaller by reducing the quantity of each ingredient by 50 to 75 percent.

SUPPLIES

To make one Apple Pendant

Completed Apple Half
(see page 67)

Headpin

Wire cutters

Round-nose pliers

Jump ring

Chain or string

1 Insert a metal headpin through the center of the bottom of your apple and pull until its head is flush with the wool. Use wire cutters to snip off the excess, leaving about ¼"/6.4mm exposed.

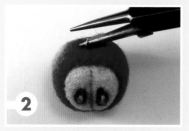

2 Using a pair of round-nose pliers, curl the exposed end of the headpin into a small loop.

3 Attach your pendant to a chain or string using a metal jump ring.

KEY CHAINS OR TOTE CHARMS

By adding a simple jump ring and clasp, any food can be made into a key chain or tote charm, which are perfect projects for trying out different sizes. Feel free to experiment and try out different amounts of the ingredients.

INGREDIENTS

To make one Rocket Pop Key Chain

Completed Rocket Pop
(see page 119)

Split jump ring

Lobster clasp

Needle and thread color to match the cherry layer of your Rocket Pop

1 pinch of Red wool

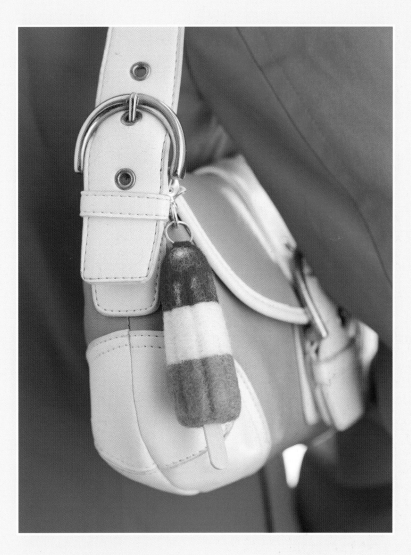

1 Attach the split jump ring to the lobster clasp.

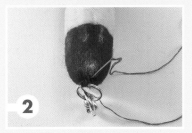

2 Using red thread, sew the jump ring onto the top of your piece.

3 Cover the sewn area with a little wool and carefully felt it down.

PINS

You can easily make most of our projects into a fashionable, quirky brooch. Just make sure there's a relatively flat space on the back of your food where you can add a simple pin back. Pin backs can be found at any fabric store or craft supplier.

SUPPLIES

To make one Watermelon Pin

Completed Watermelon Slice (see page 82)

1 pin back

Needle and thread (color to match the flesh of your watermelon)

1 tuft of blended wool (Rose and Marigold)

1 Open the pin and put a dab of E-6000 craft adhesive on the pin back.

2 Position the pin on the back of your watermelon and sew it into place.

3 To cover the exposed back of the pin, take a small tuft of blended wool and gently felt it into place.

HEADBANDS

Any food with a flat back or bottom can become a fun fascinator.

SUPPLIES

To make one Valentine's Lollipop Headband

Completed Valentine's Lollipop (see page 113)

Craft felt (color to match your lollipop)

Pencil

Elastic headband

E-6000 craft adhesive

Needle, thread, and embroidery floss (color to match your lollipop)

Scissors

Trace the outline of your heart lollipop onto a piece of craft felt.

Attach an elastic headband to the back of your lollipop, first by using a small amount of craft adhesive, then by sewing it into place with matching thread.

Carefully cut out the craft felt shape you traced in Step 1 about ¼"/6.4mm inside the line. Position the craft-felt heart over the elastic on the back of your lollipop, sew it into place with floss, then gently felt it for extra security.

133

Decorate!

MAGNETS

You can turn almost any of the foods into magnets. Just make sure there's a flat edge on the back and that your magnet is strong enough to support the food's weight. Decrease the size of the food you choose by using 50 to 75 percent of the wool called for in the original recipe.

SUPPLIES

To make one Bacon Strip Magnet

Completed Bacon Strip (see page 31)

Scissors

Tiny but strong magnet (we recommend rare earth magnets)

E-6000 craft adhesive

1 pinch of blended wool (Brick Red, Ocher, and Scarlet)

1

Cut a small hole in the back of your project the same size and shape as the magnet, taking care not to cut through to the front of your piece. Remove the cut wool and gently felt inside the hole.

2

Put a dab of craft adhesive into the hole, insert the magnet, then cover the magnet with a tuft of blended wool. Carefully felt the wool until the magnet is completely hidden.

PAPERWEIGHTS

Larger foods can easily be turned into paperweights. Choose one that has a broad base where you can add the BBs to give it heft on the bottom. We chose the Cup o' Joe, but the Cupcake or Cheeseburger would make great paperweights too.

SUPPLIES

To make one Cup o' Joe Paperweight

Completed Cup o' Joe (see page 59)

Scissors

BBs

1 gram of blended wool (Taupe and Pale Yellow)

Cut an X shape 1"/2.5cm square into the bottom of the cup. Taking care not to poke through to the outside, felt inside the X to create a small pocket.

Carefully fill the pocket with as many BBs as it can hold, pressing gently with your fingers as you go to make sure the pocket is filled.

Cover the opening with the blended wool and gently felt until the opening is securely sealed.

WALL HANGINGS

Try this project once you're comfortable freestyling with your needle-felting skills. Any food will work with these instructions.

SUPPLIES

To make one Peach Wall Hanging

6"/15.2cm embroidery hoop

Wool ingredients for the project of your choice (we chose a Peach)

½ yard/45.7cm of lightweight cotton or linen fabric

Ribbon

Pencil

Embroidery floss (optional)

1

Remove the inner ring from the embroidery hoop. Lay the ring on top of your fabric, trace around the outside edge of the hoop, then cut out the circle, leaving about 1"/2.5cm all the way around. Lightly sketch where the felted food will go within the circle.

Tip Try adding several types of felted fruit to the same fabric to make a greenmarket wall hanging.

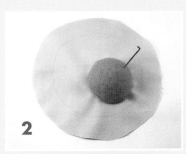

2

Place the wool in the spot you sketched out and begin to felt it into shape, making sure to felt all the way through the fabric. Once the wool begins to cling to the fabric, secure it by turning the whole piece over, laying a tuft of matching wool over the back of the felted piece, and felting until flat.

3

Finish all the details on the felt before stretching your fabric in your embroidery hoop, then erase any visible pencil lines. Tie a small loop of ribbon at the top of your hoop for easy hanging. For a finishing touch, embellish with embroidery.

PINCUSHIONS

Most of the foods can be turned into a pincushion. Our example uses the Root Beer Float, since it's in a glass and, therefore, already a bit heavier than some of the other projects.

SUPPLIES

To make one Root Beer Float Pincushion

Completed Root Beer Float (see page 53)

Pins

This one's easy—just add pins!

CENTERPIECES

Dressing up your holiday table is as quick as a hop, skip, and a jump with this charming use of our Easter Bunnies.

SUPPLIES

To make one Easter Bunny Centerpiece

Completed Chocolate Bunnies (see page 115)

Floral foam

Basket

Excelsior or shredded paper

Wooden skewers cut to 4"/10.2cm

E-6000 craft adhesive

Tufts of wool to match the projects (for wrapping the tops of the skewers)

Additional embellishments (optional)

1 Place the block of foam in your basket. Use the shredded paper or excelsior around the edges of the foam to wedge it in place.

2 Dab glue on the cut end of a skewer and wrap it with wool. Cut a small hole in the bottom of the bunny, insert the skewer, and felt around it carefully to secure it.

3 Arrange the bunnies as desired by inserting the skewers into the foam. Use excelsior or shredded paper to fill in the arrangement and cover any exposed foam.

PLACE CARD HOLDERS

Anything with a flat bottom can become an adorable place card holder. Imagine the possibilities at a wedding—or your next dinner party or buffet table.

SUPPLIES

To make one Frosted Cake Slice Place Card Holder

Completed Frosted Cake Slice (see page 97)

20-gauge wire

Wire cutters

Round-nose pliers

Heavyweight paper

Writing instrument of choice

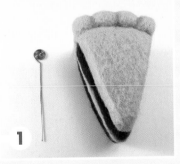

1

Cut an 8"/20.3cm piece of 20-gauge wire using your wire cutters. Using a pair of round-nose pliers, curl about 4"/10.2cm of the wire into a spiral.

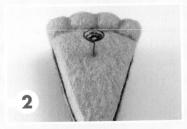

2

Insert the wire into your needle-felted project. Gently press the center of your spiral forward to separate the wire coils slightly.

3

Print or write your message on a piece of heavyweight paper and insert the paper between the coils of the spiral.

ORNAMENTS

Any of our projects are happy to hang around with you. Adding a hanging ribbon loop is a quick and easy task.

SUPPLIES

To make one Gingerbread Man Ornament

Completed Iced Gingerbread Man (see page 127)

8"/20.3cm of ribbon

1 tuft of wool (we used Pelsull Ocher for the Gingerbread Man)

Scissors

Broken needle or toothpick

1 Fold the ribbon in half and tie the two ends in a knot. Wrap the knot in a tuft of Pelsull Ocher wool and carefully felt the tuft to the ribbon, needling gently through the ribbon as you work.

2 Cut a small hole in the top of your needle-felted project. Use a broken needle or a toothpick to push the woolly end of the ribbon into the hole, then carefully felt the ribbon loop into place.

Tip

Gingerbread men ornaments also make excellent holiday gift box embellishments.

Resources

When you're looking for wool and other needle-felting supplies, in addition to arts and crafts stores you should look in local yarn stores and at farmers markets. Keep your eyes open for sheep and wool festivals, too—those gatherings are gold mines for great wool. We've listed some resources here that will help you find wool, needles, foam blocks, kits, and more. You can also try a keyword search on your favorite online marketplace, and lots of good things will pop up. There are plenty of great video resources out there too. If you find yourself needing visual instruction, scout out tutorials online

WOOL & SUPPLIES

AMERICAN FELT AND CRAFT
www.americanfeltandcraft.com
• This is a great resource for prefelt and tools.

CLOVER
www.clover-usa.com
•This is the company that sells our favorite multi-needle tool.

HI-FIBER KITS
www.etsy.com/shop/hifiberkits
• Offers a good selection of wool and other goodies.

KAY PETAL
www.needlefeltingsupplies.com
• She has lots of videos and tutorials on her website.

KERRI WESSEL
www.fuzzefood.com
• Kerri sells kits and supplies.

LIVING FELT
www.livingfelt.com
A great selection of wool and tools.

NEW ENGLAND FELTING SUPPLY
www.feltingsupply.com
• New England Felting Supply is the store where Kari worked when she and Kerri met! They sell all kinds of wool and supplies, including all of the colors we used in this book.

The following stores can be found throughout the United States (Jo-Ann and Michaels stores are also in Canada), and all of them carry needle-felting supplies. Check your local listings or online for locations near you.

A. C. MOORE
www.acmoore.com

HOBBY LOBBY
www.hobbylobby.com

JO-ANN FABRIC AND CRAFT
www.joann.com

MICHAELS STORES
www.michaels.com

FELLOW FAB NEEDLE FELTERS

Needle felting can be used to make lots of different kinds of projects. Here are some websites of folks out there who are using the medium to make amazing things.

CHRISSY MAHUNA
www.thefeltedchicken.com

JACKIE HUANG
www.woolbuddy.com

LEBRIE RICH
www.penfelt.com

LIZ SMITH
www.madeinlowell.com

MOXIE
www.ifeltawesome.com

Acknowledgments

We dedicated this book to our family and friends, and we would like to thank them again here. Their support proved to be invaluable while we created this book for you. We'd like to illuminate the following people and thank them publicly for their influence and help: Holly Bemiss, Maeg Yosef, Chris Gugliotti, Stephen Andrade, Eric Nixon, Pete, Odin, Puppy, Baxter, and Charlie Parker and Zoe, and all of the fine people at Sixth&Spring.

Index